The Book of Jared

The Book of Jared

Jared Hampton

GroundWorks Management LLC

Copyright info

Printed in the United States of America

All rights reserved to the Author. No part of this publication may be reproduced, distributed, or transmitted in any form or by any means, including photocopying, recording, or other electronic or mechanical methods, without the prior written permission of the publisher, except in the case of brief quotations embodied in critical reviews and commercial uses permitted by copyright law. For permission requests, write to the publisher, addressed "Attention: Permissions Coordinator," at the address below.

ISBN: 978-1-7350262-2-0 (Paperback)

ISBN: 978-1-7350262-3-7 (Ebook)

Biblical context and quotation is taken from New King James Version

Publishing Company: GroundWorks Management LLC

JARED HAMPTON

P.O. Box 241225
Chicago IL, 60624
Business   Email: groundworksmgmtllc@gmail.com

Introduction

"To the twelve tribes which are scattered abroad: Greetings (James 1:1 NKJV)." First off, I would like to thank the Most High for putting me through the suffering, the test and the disciplining that caused me to search deep within myself and learn my true nature and look to Him for all my help. Ephesians 6:12 is a commonly known bible verse. "For we do not wrestle against the flesh and blood, but against principalities, against powers, against the rulers of the darkness of this age, against spiritual wickedness in the heavenly places (New King James Version)." We've all heard this scripture, but how seriously do we take it? Do we know how spiritual warfare manifest itself in our physical day to day? Do we know how to bind a demonic or unclean spirit? Do we know how to engage the enemy with the sword, and not just always hold up the shield? Do we know how to deliver ourselves from strongholds and break generational curses? Do we believe in the administration of angels? Do we know how to use our angels? I definitely did not. I grew up in church my whole life but didn't learn the essential and lifesaving skills of spiritual warfare until 2019. We call these things stress, anxiety, depression, suicidal thoughts, rage, disease and many other man-made disorders. I was faced with all sorts of unbelievable, strange phenomena happening to me and I couldn't just "give it to Jesus" or "pray it away." I had to fight, but not with physical weapons, but with the sword of Truth. Colossians 3:16 says "Let the word of Ha'Mashiach (Christ) dwell in you richly in all wisdom, teaching, and admonishing one another in psalms and hymns and spiritual songs, singing with grace in your hearts to Yahuah (the Lord) (NKJV)." This book is my gift to you the reader, for wisdom, teaching and admonishment through the gift that was given to me through my test of faith. My prayer is that you are blessed by it and your connection to the father, Yah, is established, strengthened, and made alive. May you prosper and be in good health, just as your soul prospers. All praise to the Most High!

Psalms 1
(Lamentation)

Haven't been a good friend
I haven't been a good man
Show me where I said I was?
Behind the curtain I blame myself
Backstage they say I messed up my lines
In the meeting I messed up the project
The love I give apparently is not good.
The friendship I give not valued
I used to understand myself
I used to forgive myself
I had compassion on myself
Now I stand in the judgment
I'm sure the accuser of our brothers was accusing me today.
Did I curse the name of Elohiym?
Do I sin when I say I am not a Christian?

Why am I forsaken? Why am I outcast?

My heart is heavy within me. My spirit broken.

Laughter escapes me. A spirit of despair is on me. A spirit of hopelessness.

My tree produces no fruit. I am laughed at and mocked in the city for my failures.

Another person lives in my house and another man has what was mine.

Your Hand is heavy on me Lord. Who can bare it?

How long will you be angry with me Yah?

How long will you withhold your grace and mercy from me?

Trouble finds me in the morning and heartbreak creeps into my dreams at night. Who is Jared that you think of me?

What do you require of me that you give me the breath of life and my daily bread? My bed is soaked with my tears.

I turn my plate down in discouragement.

What wickedness have you found in my heart?

What darkness keeps you from my presence?

Show me this darkness so that I may shine light on it.

Show me this wickedness so that I may confess my sin and seek righteousness. Then Elohiym will come into my heart again.

He will love me as a Father loves his son

He will restore my strength and renew my joy.

My joy will be full like a cup overflowing because Yah will be the center of my joy. Peace will be with me when I ly down secure in my bed.

Wisdom and Understanding will be my sister and kinswoman in the day.

Lord, please forgive my sins. Do not delay to help me.

Psalms 2

Those who are jealous of me slander my name.

Because I do not do as they wish, I am counted among the wicked.

My enemies lay in the shadows anxiously waiting to see me fall.

They long to say "Aha! See! I knew he was not a righteous man. He does not fear Elohiym."

Why does my enemy raise the sword to me when I have dropped the shield?

Why does my enemy pursue me when I do not flee?

My enemy has laid a case before the courthouse of the Ancient of Days.

He has accused me like the accuser of our brothers who accuses day and night.

He that is without sin, cast the first stone!

Who are you to judge another man's servant?

Have we not all sinned?

THE BOOK OF JARED

Have I hidden my sins from our Heavenly Abba?

Has the Most High's eyes not seen what I have done?

Has El Shaddai not have His awesome and powerful hand on me when I was in the dark?

Where can I hide my deceit from His knowledge?

There is no place for this son of Abraham to hide.

If I go to Sheol You are there.

If I hide in the skies, you are there.

No there is no place for me to go.

My sins are laid bare before the eyes of Yahuah.

He will judge me for everything I do, my short days under the sun.

And in His great mercy He will forgive me if I sincerely repent and turn from sin.

I am no longer a slave to sin but a slave to righteousness.

I no longer walk in the darkness; the Law of Yah is an overflow of light to my heart.

Show grace and compassion to your servant Jared.

My enemies attack me, while I sleep in my tent at peace.

One night my enemy prays for me and the next day they attack me with my guard down.

Is this justice?

Is this righteous?

I will not be like the Pharisee who said thank Yah that I am not sinful like the tax collector.

Nay, I am a sinner. Forgive me Yah. I beat my chest and tear my clothes.

As David told Saul, may Yah judge between me and my enemies.

Psalms 3

Many seek Wisdom but only few are able to find her.

She is not a one-night stand.

She is not a cheap date.

Wisdom will test you with her requirements until she trust you are worthy.

She cannot be downloaded or bought.

She has to be earned.

Thanks be to Yah, that He has given us the first step to her.

To fear Yah is wisdom, to turn from doing evil is understanding.

The Law of Elohiym makes the simple wise.

If you delight in His commands, it will be a light unto your feet and a lamp to your path.

What do you have against the Law of Elohiym son of man?

Do you want to deceive your brother?

Do you want to slander your sister?

Do you want to withhold wages from one who has earned them?

Do you want to murder, steal and commit adultery?

If not, then what do you have in you that is against the Law?

The Law is not burdensome. His yoke is easy, and His burden is light.

Wisdom is found all throughout the law that was given to Mosheh (Moses).

Search your heart my brother. Search your soul my sister.

You say you desire wisdom, but you reject the commands of Elohiym.

That is why you are foolish.

Psalms 4

Resist the devil and he will flee from you.

Embrace him and he will devour you.

Truly the man who fears Yah avoids all extremes.

And likewise, the man who indulges in the desires of the flesh will find calamity.

Distress and despair will never be too far from his heart.

He has not yet discovered that the devil is a con artist. A scammer.

What he offers is cheap because it is counterfeit.

His gifts are pretty packages with fine decor and a scorpion waits on the inside.

Children there is nothing good he has to offer.

He was a liar from the beginning and the truth is not in him.

He is lawlessness.

Test the spirits.

All good and perfect gifts come from Yahuah.

He is able to give us exceedingly above and beyond all we could ever desire.

Therefore, put your faith in Him.

Which of you if your child asks for bread would give him a stone?

If you (being evil), know how to give good gifts.

How much better gifts will your Father give you?

Psalms 5

When I wake up in the morning, I seek the presence of Yah.

Before I check for likes and followers, I pray to the Most High and thank Him for His love.

He has loved me with an everlasting love and drawn me with an unfailing kindness.

I inquired of myself "how long son of Jacob will you be at war with Elohiym?"

How often have I said, "I feel like I am at war with my Creator, who can save me?" I was the clay saying to the potter "what are you doing?"

Then I said, I have been stiff-necked and stubborn like my ancestors before me. I have loved the things of the world more than the things of Elohiym.

I have forgotten my first works that I had when I first loved Him.

Now I say you are the potter, and I am the clay.

All of us are works of His hands.

I likened being molded as to one going through growing pains.

It may hurt during the process but remember you are getting taller.

And as you get taller you see things from a higher perspective.

A higher dimension, the level on which the Spirit moves.

As gold is tested by fire, He has tested my heart in the furnace of affliction.

But I learned from my ancestor Job not to curse his name or claim self-righteousness.

He has led me through the wilderness to test me, to see what is in my heart.

And has found that I will keep His commands!

Now I laugh at danger. I know who goes out before me when my enemy attacks. Where would I be without the mercy of my Father?

How could I survive, in this evil world without the Living Elohiym protecting me? His justice is stronger than white supremacy.

His providence is greater than mass incarceration.

His love teaches me not to be physically, verbally or emotionally abusive.

He does not manipulate me into loving Him.

He cares for the poor, the widow and the orphan.

The foreigner who fears Him, He will not reject.

He is an Elohiym of justice. He hates dishonest scales.

He hates those who withhold wages from a worker. I find courage in Yah.

He has been with me since I was a child at my mother's knee.

He has told me who I was before I ever got a degree, diploma, or job title.

He has shown me that I am counted among the sons of Elohiym.

I have made Yahusha my brother by my faith in Him and keeping our Father's commands. What can man do to me? I will not fear man

I have put my trust in Yah. My foot will not dash against a stone.

Psalms 6

How dare any evil spirit or principality stand against me!

Do you not know?

Yahusha has given me power and authority to trample on snakes and scorpions and to overcome all the power of the enemy.

Not some but all!

Nothing can harm me.

I crush fierce lions and serpents under my feet!

I am bold as a lion.

My hand is on the neck of my enemies. Like a lion I crouch and ly down.

Who dares to rouse me?

The Elohiym of peace has bruised satan under my feet.

The Spirit that was given to me commands me to be powerful, loving and self controlled.

THE BOOK OF JARED

I am so bold that I even ask the messengers He sent me, are you for me or against me?

I put my foot on the necks of these kings!

I told satan to get behind me! You do not have on your mind the concerns of Elohiym but merely human concerns.

You are cast into the lake of fire son of the morning.

You have accused the last of our brothers you false witness.

You have fallen from Shamayim like lightning because you said to yourself, I will be like the Most High.

There is only one Elohiym.

Who can say to him "what have you done?"

On the day He returns and unleashes his wrath on the wicked, who can say to him "that is enough!"

He shows mercy to those he chooses and compassion to those He loves.

He exalts the humble and humbles those who exalt themselves.

He will stop by a brook and drink from it.

He will bend Judah like a bow and fill it with Ephraim.

Why do you doubt Israel, why are you afraid Judah?

Is Yah's arm too short?

Take shelter under his wings. Make Him your refuge.

Have courage and do not fear.

If Elohiym be for us, who can be against us?

Psalms 7

It is written, man shall not live off bread alone but by every word that proceed from the mouth of Elohiym

There is a famine in my inner parts when I do not read your word.

My spirit growls with hunger pains

I cook a meal of the best foods and eat til my heart's content, but I am still hungry.

My wife brings me breakfast in bed, but if she does not bring me a morning word, I am still hungry.

The bread of life is the word of Elohiym.

When I do not eat of this bread or drink from this cup, my spirit is sick and injured.

Just as food is strength for the body so is the word of Elohiym strength for the soul.

Eat of the word when you wake up young man.

Have a feast of psalms and proverbs in the evening before you sleep young woman.

There is no overeating when it comes to the word of Elohiym.

Yah will delight in you when your appetite is for His word.

You will find His word is better than any food.

Psalms 8

I have been given authority to trample on snakes and scorpions.

It was commanded of me that I should overcome all the power of the enemy.

Praise Yah!

I searched for my Heavenly Abba in my house.

He was not there.

I looked for Him in my car and at my job.

He could not be found.

I looked in my bank account and social media profiles.

I did not see His face.

Then I said, Elohiym is not there.

He does not show himself to the sinner.

Then I said "I will look for Him in my heart"

And it is there I found him!

For the kingdom of Elohiym is in the hearts of man and woman.

Is it not written, the Spirit he caused to dwell within us?

Is it not written that He has given us of His spirit?

Search for Yah in your heart and you will find Him.

Look for him as you would when you have lost your keys.

Pursue him young man as you would a pretty girl who caught your eye.

You will find His reward is 1000 times greater than anything she could give.

As eagerly as you wait in line to get into the club.

Wait on Yahuah!

Wait patiently for El Shaddai.

He will restore your strength and you will mount up with wings like an eagle.

You will walk through the floods and shall not drown

You will walk through the fire and will not be burned.

No weapon formed against you shall prosper.

For such is the inheritance of those who serve Elohiym.

Psalms 9

A righteous man falls down 7 times and will still get up.

The wicked fall and there is no help for them

The man who delights in the Law of Elohiym is not easily moved.

The commands of Yah are like sweet honey in his mouth.

The precepts and statutes of the Most High are more beautiful to him than 100 virgins.

The fear of Yah has replaced the fear of the world and the flesh in his heart.

For once you feel the fear of Elohiym all other fear is irrational and irrelevant.

The man who seeks Yah with his whole heart will be rewarded for his commitment.

Not that he should count his works as righteousness.

But that his obedience to the commands and faith in Yahusha have made him a new man.

Psalms 10 (We do) – Sacred wedding vows.

We do not manipulate one another.
We do not blame one another.
We do not deceive one another.
We do not shame one another.
We do not punish one another.
We do not teach each other a lesson.
We do not dismiss one another.
We do not passive aggressively attack one another.
We do not give each other the silent treatment.
We do not curse at one another
We do not scream at one another
We do not trade insult for insult.
We do not trade blow for blow.
We do not harm one another.

THE BOOK OF JARED

We do not hurt one another.
We do not return evil for evil.
We do not try to control one another.
We do not deal treacherously with one another.
We do not deal harshly with one another.
We are not mean to one another.
We do show each other mercy.
We do show each other compassion.
We do actively listen to one another.
We do show each other grace.
We do forgive one another.
We do show empathy to one another.
We do show understanding to one another.
We do trust one another.
We do protect each other emotionally
We do protect each other spiritually.
We do pray for one another.
We do respect one another.

We do create a safe environment for one another.

We do allow each other to be an individual.
We do both submit to Yah.
We do both study scripture on our own and together.

We do both speak kindly to one another.

We do show self-accountability for our actions.

We do take full responsibility for our actions despite "what the other person did."

We do show remorse and apologize when we disappoint or upset the other person.

We do build each other up.

We do encourage one another.

We do show patience with one another.

We are nice to one another.

We do keep Yah first in ALL things we say and do.

We do practice the law, statutes and commandments.

We do love each other as Yahusha loved us.

We do give charity to one another.

We do live our lives and marriage to be an example of how two people glorify Elohiym and give him godly offspring.

We do not use I did this because you did something first as an excuse for us choosing to respond abusively after an offense.

We are humble towards one another.

We do defend one another when we are right.

We do hold one another accountable when we are wrong.

We do glorify Elohiym in everything we do.

We do not curse at one another. Cursing is witchcraft.

We do not damage each other's property.

We do not hold grudges.

We do not embarrass each other.

We do not humiliate each other.

We do not mistreat one another.

We do not torture one another.

We do not harass one another.

We do not mock one another.

We do not intimidate one another.

We do not abuse one another.

We do support one another.

We do heal one another.

We do replenish one another.

We do help each other recover.

We do care for one another.

We do edify one another.

We do coach each other.

We do improve each other.

We do elevate Elohiym first then we elevate each other.

We do guide one another with Elohiym's help.

We do not have nasty attitudes with one another.

We do not try to "get even" with each other when upset.

We do pray together.

We do guard each other's hearts.

We do treat each other with dignity and civility.

We do not try to "discipline" one another.

We do tremble at the word of Elohiym

We do serve our community

We do accept correction without being defensive or deflecting.

We do not avenge when one has offended the other.

We do nothing out of selfish ambition or vain conceit

We are selfless not selfish.

We do not abandon ourselves.

We do not abandon each other.

We do make one another feel safe

We do not leave each other hanging

THE BOOK OF JARED

We are faithful and loyal to one another.

We do not commit adultery

We do not cheat emotionally

We do not hide things from each other

We do not keep secrets

We do not betray one another's trust

We do not speak recklessly or rashly to one another.

We do not interrupt each other when one is talking.

We do let the other finish their thought completely.

We do not talk over one another.

We do correct our behavior the first time after we apologize.

We do not make one another jealous

We do set and enforce boundaries

We do not use force, threats or intimidation to get a point across

We do not treat each other with hostility

We do not engage in violence against one another

We do not use what we've learned about psychology, religion and human behavior as a means to show off or exalt ourselves.

We do use what we've learned about psychology, religion and human behavior as a means to help one another heal.

We do practice justice with one another.

We do not love one another in the Euro-centric/western romanticize version of love.

We do love by showing mercy, compassion, empathy, forgiveness, grace, loyalty, faithfulness and charity to one another.

We do!

Psalms 11

To not sin is to practice the Law, because sin is lawlessness.

You say you do not sin, inherently you say I practice the Law.

To practice the Law, is to practice not sinning.

Why are you afraid of his word child of Elohiym?

His commands are not burdensome.

They make the simple wise and give understanding to the foolish man.

If Elohiym doesn't want it then I don't want it.

I'm trying to live my life in a way that emulates my Father.

I want to be more like Yahusha. More like the Most High.

Do not keep yourself small or hidden to please others.

That is a command! That's an order!

Do not be afraid to say NO.
That is a command! That's an order.
Do not be afraid to ask for what you want.
That is a command! That's an order.
I do not want to be charming in the way I have in the past.
You charm a snake. Do you want to live forever with a snake?
I want to use my charm for righteousness.
Charm is deceptive.

Psalms 12 (I AM)

I am a servant of the Most High God.
I am a son of God.
I am a great man.
I am a lion.
I am a warrior.
I am a problem solver.
I am not finished.
I am a teacher.
I am not defeated.
I am power.
I am a conqueror.
I am redeemed.
I am a brother of Yahusha Ha'Mashiach.
I am a man of integrity.
I am not a quitter.
I am a finisher.
I am not a liar.
I am not a people pleaser.

I am a man.
I am a god. (Psalm 82:6)
I am a son of Abraham.
I am justified.
I am glorified.
I am called for His purpose.
I am a creator.
I am a father.
I am a husband.
I am a priest.
I am a defender of the widow, the fatherless and the poor.
I am like my Heavenly Father, Yahuah.

Psalms 13

Know for certain that you are being protected and not punished my children.

You are being built up and not broken.

You are being healed and not harmed.

You are being praised and not persecuted.

You are being empowered and not enslaved.

You are redeemed not rebuked.

You are winning and not losing.

You are being remembered not forgotten.

He has not forgotten you.

You have forgotten that Yah has always watched over you and provided you with your every need.

He has always walked with me. He has always been there for me.

All of my help has always come from Yahuah.

Psalms 14
(Lamentation 2)

I fall down on my knees.

I ask my God please.

Do not let me be forsaken.

For your namesake you rescued Israel time and time again.

Am I not a child of Jacob?

Am I not a son of Abraham?

Why then do you hide your face from me?

Why have you not shown favor to your servant?

My soul is downcast within me.

I am humbled and my spirit is contrite.

Against you and you alone have I sinned.

I have dealt treacherously with the wife of my youth.

I have not drunk water from my own cistern.

I have dealt harshly with the one I should protect.

I put her away.

Forgive me Father.

Have mercy on me according to thy tender mercies.

I have not loved her as I love myself.

I have not washed her with the word.

She too is a daughter of Abraham.

She is a daughter of Sarah.

Have mercy on us.

Have compassion on our souls.

We did not love one another as Christ loved us.

We trusted in things of the world to guide us.

We trusted in therapy and counseling more than prayer and repentance.

We trusted in doctors more than we trusted in the Holy Spirit.

What can the gardener say to the mechanic about how to fix a car?

Even more, what can the counselor say to the Holy Spirit about how to fix a soul?

I am a spirit with a body. I love and worship in spirit.

The counselor does not know what to say to me.

The Holy Spirit does.

Psalms 15

Yah's grace is sufficient for me.

God's grace is sufficient for me.

His power is made perfect in my weakness.

Yah's power is made perfect in my weakness.

Where I am weak, He is strong.

Where I am lacking, He compensates for me.

When I don't know everything, He knows everything.

When I don't know what to say He knows what to say.

When I am tired, He does not tire. Does the Lord sleep?

When I fall down, He is there to pick me up.

Like a good Shepherd tending His sheep.

He calls my name and I listen.

He looks for me when I am lost.

When I fall and cut myself, He is a compassionate Father. He binds my wounds.

He cares for me like a loving Father cares for his children.

When I make the wrong decisions, He speaks to me and shows me my error.

He corrects me because He has accepted me as a son.

I am not an illegitimate child.

When He gives me work to do, I do it gladly.

Like any son I want to make my Father proud.

I want to be more like my Heavenly Father everyday.

I don't live my life in fear because I know my Father will protect me.

I know my Father will never leave me nor forsake me.

I know my Father loves me.

That is why I am able to stand.

No man cannot hinder me.

Psalms 16

I thought I knew the way in which I should go.

I thought I knew what and who to pray for.

I thought I understood things that all men did not.

I thought that my faith could move mountains.

I thought that I was highly esteemed.

I am just a man.

There is nothing special about me among the sons of women.

I used to be counted among the wise.

Now I am counted amongst the fools.

People came from far and wide to take counsel from me.

Now they say, "this man lacks understanding why ask him anything?"

My enemy camps outside my tent.

He sees that I am vulnerable, and the Lord has found fault in me.

The townspeople say, He trusted in God, let God save him now.

For thy namesake, will you let a son of Israel be mocked by these godless people?

Will a slave rule over the freeborn sons of Abraham?

Can the dead praise the living God?

Most High God restore me for my home has been raided by thieves.

They have moved ancient boundary stones from around my dwelling.

They slander my name and bring false charges against me.

Who can save me?

El Shaddai who has been my refuge since a boy will.

Not for my namesake but for your covenant with your servant Jacob you preserve me.

It was you who taught Ephraim how to walk; it was you who healed him.

Teach me to be upright and walk in your ways.

Have mercy on me according to thy tender mercies, which are new each morning.

My God, My God, do not forsake me.

Psalms 17 (Praise in the midst of the storm)

What am I supposed to do?
What can I do?
There is nothing I can do now.
My faith is really being tested.
All before I thought I held all the power.
Now that power has been stripped from me.
I cannot find my way home.
I do not know the way to my heart.
There is nothing I can do.
Except trust in Yah... Now all that trust talk is being put to the test.

Now all that prayer and faith is being put to the test.

If you trust Yahuah, what are you worried about?

Why are you crying? Why are you dismayed?

Is it not written, do not fear, for I am with you.

Do not be dismayed, for I am your God. I will strengthen you and help you.

I will uphold you with my righteous right hand.

This is where the rubber meets the road.

In order to have something you never had you have to do something you never did.

This is definitely new territory for me.

Whatever His will is, His will for me for others is greater than my will for myself.

His plans for me are greater than my plans for myself.

And His love for me is far more abundant, forgiving and compassionate than my love for myself.

His faithfulness to me is greater than my faithfulness to myself.

HalleluYah! HalleluYah! HalleluYah!

Holy Holy Holy is the Lord God Almighty.

Who was, and is and is to come.

Yahusha told me not to worry for I am worth more than sparrows or lilies.

Restore in me a clean heart O God. Create in me an upright spirit to sustain me.

You are worthy, Yahuah our Elohiym, to receive glory honor and power.

For you created all things, and by your will they were created and have their being.

Create in me a clean and obedient heart.

Create in me a steadfast and upright spirit.

Give me peace that surpasses all understanding.

Hope and faith that makes people look at me like a madman.

When everything seems to be falling apart, I am celebrating the victory!

I am walking around looking and feeling good.

My stomach is full of choice food and moderate wine.

My face is shining as I've anointed myself with oil.

The unbelievers say, "why does he look this way when he has lost so much?"

It is because I keep the faith and trust in Yah Is not just a saying.

It's a command! It's a way of life. It's an inheritance. It's an insurance policy!

That when I mess up. And I get my soul in an accident He is my insurance!

And insurance pays for what I messed up!

Don't believe me!? The Holy Spirit is a deposit to guarantee great things that are to come!

When I mess up at the job, He's my insurance!

When I mess up with my family, He's my insurance policy!

When I wreck my heart in relationships and friendships, He is my insurance!!!

And what is my deductible, a contrite spirit; a broken and humbled heart God will not turn away.

Like a good neighbor, the Holy Spirit is there!

Is there a witness!?

Not for me, but for His namesake!

He restores my soul, He guides me on the paths of righteousness. For His name's sake!

Thank you Yahuah!

Thank you Yahusha!

When my Father sees me, He sees Yahusha Ha'Mashiach (Jesus Christ). He sees his precious blood not my filthy rags.

I worship you with my whole heart, mind, body and soul Yah.

I ask you to restore my soul and guide me on the righteous path in accordance with your will! Forever!

Psalms 18

Weeping may endure for a night, but joy comes in the morning.

I wept.

What does crying have to do with the body?

The eyes are just a tool.

When our innermost being is bruised.

When the Spirit that dwells within us, in the inner parts is wounded.

When our soul is hurting beyond physical comprehension.

We cry.

And our tears reach the feet of the Almighty God.

Its easy how we can forget how bitter our tears tasted.

Its easy to forget how bad someone made us feel.

Its easy to forget that someone you loved and trusted is the one who made you cry.

I wept. I cried hard.

I poured out my heart to Lord Almighty.

In my spirit I was unraveled. I was abused. I was beat down. I was mistreated. Its easy to forget.

But our Heavenly Father does not forget the tears we have cried.

Every drop is counted. He feels our pain.

Yahusha knows what we are going through.

Our high priest does empathize with us.

Why then son of man, would he lead his sheep back to the wolf?

Why then son of man, would he dry your tears then lead you back to the source of them.

No. That's not what a good Father would do.

A good Father protects you from those who would harm you.

A good Shepherd protects his sheep from the wolf.

I love my Heavenly Father, Yahuah.

When I was in distress and did cry painful tears, He dried my eyes.

When I was in despair and did weep, He picked me up as if I was a small child.

He held me in His arms and said, there there now, it will be alright.

When I was ready to take my life, He sheltered me under His wings. He sheltered me from death.

He said, I still have a future for you. A future with hope and prosperity and peace.

When we cry, our spirit is talking to its Father. Talking to its creator.

He has not forgotten my tears.

He will not lead me back to more.

Psalms 19

Lean not on your own understanding but TRUST in Yahuah with all your heart.

In all your ways submit to Him, and He will make your paths straight.

Yahuah is my strength and my shield; in him my heart TRUSTS

Those who KNOW YOUR NAME put their TRUST in you, O Yahuah.

I am not afraid of receiving any bad news. My heart is firm, I TRUST in Yahuah.

My mind stays on Him and I am in perfect peace because I TRUST Him.

All things work together for my good not some things ALL things!

I commit my ways, how I live my life to Yahuah. I TRUST Him and He acts on my behalf.

HalleluYah!

He acts on my behalf!

The Lord himself, Yah, acts on my behalf!
Praise God!

I am like a tree planted by the water. I do not fear when the heat is on because I TRUST in the Lord Almighty.

When I am afraid I put my TRUST in Him.

I have put my TRUST in You Yah. Show me the way I should go. I TRUST you with my life!

I live by faith and not by sight.

Yahuah is my Helper. I am not afraid. What can man do to me?

I am waiting on the Lord, Yah. I have decided to be strong and take heart.

I hope for what I do not yet have, and I wait patiently for it.

My hope is not in vain. My faith is not in vain.

My heart leaps for joy because I TRUST Him. He helps me out.

I am eager to see the goodness and the glory of Yah in the land of the living!

Psalms 20 (Yah repairs)

Those who are well are in no need of a physician.

Show me what is broken, and I will fix it.

Yahuah is near the brokenhearted and saves those who are crushed in spirit.

Bring the Potter all the broken pots, so that He may restore them and make them new!

Behold! He makes all things new. Bring me the broken pieces!

What is there for me to do with those who are already righteous or whole?

Bring me the broken parts!

How can I put together what is already assembled?

I rejoice for the broken and shattered parts

They count me as a madman. The prophet is considered a fool.

The spiritual man is mad.

How can I show my skill as a repairman on something that is already repaired?

I love the broken things!

It is in our weakness that His strength is made perfect.

His grace is sufficient for us!

How could he save us if we did not need rescuing?

How could Yahusha die for our sins if we were already righteous in the eyes of Yahuah?

It takes patience and skill to fix that which was broken.

The world says "leave what is broken and needs healing as it is.

Less you might hurt yourself and find yourself in debt."

Thank Elohiym that He does not see us as we see one another.

Where would we be if He took this approach?

What if He said, "Israel is broken, why should I labor myself putting him back together?" Abraham's descendants are sick, why should I heal them?"

HalleluYah!

I will praise the God of Israel and be eternally grateful you are not like man.

Man breaks a thing and throws it away to buy something new, something better.

Where would Jacob be if you did not pick him up when he fell down?

How could Saul see if you had not restored sight to his eyes as Paul.

I will praise you Yahuah for who you are.

I will praise you Yahusha for how you have given us the only path to eternal life.

Show me the broken things!

For the Lord delights in those who are humble and contrite of spirit.

He will restore to them all they lost as He did with his servant Job.

Psalms 21 (Thank You)

Thank you Yah for another day.

Thank you Yah for waking me up this morning.

Thank you for keeping us safe from danger over the night.

Thank you, Adonai, for the beautiful day you made today.

Thank you for friends and family that love and care about me.

Thank you for being Elohiym.

Thank you for your grace and your mercy.

Thank you for your son Yahusha Ha'Mashiach who died to save me from sin.

Thank you for giving me a portion of your Holy Spirit.

I love you.

Forgive me for my sins as I forgive those who sin against me.

Forever. Amen.

Psalms 22

Today is a day that Yahuah has made.
Let us rejoice and be glad in it!
As long as it is called today
Let us encourage and support one another.
Let the children play in the street
Without fear of violence
Let their laughter fill the halls and corners of every home and school.
Dry your eyes you weeping woman.
Quiet your silent screams you hunted man.
The Lord Almighty has heard your cry.
Your tears have reached the foot of his throne daughter of Zion.
Your silent screams He has heard son of Jacob.
We are not forsaken.
We are not condemned.
We are not abandoned.

When we are distressed our Heavenly Father is in distress

That is why we ought to cast our cares upon Yahuah.

Banish all anxiety from your heart young man.

Tell Him all about your troubles young woman, for He cares for you.

Learn from Him. His yoke is easy, and His burden is light.

What is His burden?

To love the Lord, Yah, with all your heart mind body and soul and to treat your neighbor as yourself.

Psalms 23

My heart is sick and stubborn.

The heart is deceitful beyond all things

Who can understand it?

I am no better than my ancestors

I long to go back to Egypt.

I have been complaining and finding fault in everything.

Please sanctify and purify my heart Yahuah

Remove from me this heart of stone and give me a heart of flesh

Create in me an upright heart and a ruach ha'qodesh

Yahuah Ahavah Shalom bless me with an abundance of love and peace

Elohiym is righteous in all his judgments and decrees

His knowledge and wisdom are from everlasting

He alone is holy and worthy to be praised
Yah I repent from my sins.
Show mercy to your servant Jared.

According to your tender mercies, which are new, each morning.

Psalms 24

I am from a line of kings of the tribe of Yahudah (Judah)

From the tribe of David and Yahusha (Jesus).

I am a lion's cub.

I walk with a stately stride.

Like an old lion I crouch down to rest.

Who dares to rouse me?

When I seize my victim and carry it off, who will rescue them?

The righteous are bold as a lion.

The king of the animals won't turn aside for anything.

YAHUAH TSEVA'OTH stalks prey for the young lions to satisfy their appetite.

Likewise, Elohiym corners my enemy for me and gives me the victory every time!

He gave a loud shout like the roar of a lion

And I came to Him from the west.

He showed me how to hunt and survive in the wilderness.

The elders said to me, "Weep no more; behold, the Lion of the tribe of Judah, the Root of David, has conquered, so that he can open the scroll and its seven seals."

I will praise the Most High forever and ever.

Psalms 25

The angels in Shamayim love me and I love them.

Time after time His messengers that watch over me reported to Yahuah on my behalf.

When I was thinking of taking my life, the messengers said to my Adonai.

Sovereign Lord, your servant Jared is in trouble. The enemy is tempting him. Shall we go down?

And Yahuah answered, Go down to him and refresh his spirit and encourage his heart.

Clear his mind of iniquity.

And the angel came to me and did comfort me, dried my tears and cleared my mind.

When my mother was sick, and at deaths door the angel said to Yahuah

Lord Almighty, your servant Jared is in trouble. His mother is sick and needs air.

And my Lord said go down to her and fill her lungs with the breath of life.

He pitied me time and time again.

His compassion has not failed me yet.

He has chosen me among my brothers to have my hand on the neck of my enemies.

To worship and praise Him in spirit because He is Spirit.

To be a father to the fatherless and take up the cause of the widow and give to the poor.

He has shared His name with me among all my brothers.

His Spirit has led me to the truth about His son and His commandments.

I will defend the God of Israel because He has defended me.

I will not blaspheme or ever show disrespect or disdain for my Elohiym.

I do not have the heart too.

When 5 cars were flipping in front of me, I heard your voice say move left, don't brake.

When a car ran the stop sign and almost T boned my car, you caused me to look out the corner of my eye and slam on brake.

Time after time you have shown favor to your humble servant.

I love you. I worship you. I adore you. I fear you. I am your son.

You are my Abba Father

Psalms 26 (To A'dam or Adam)

I need Yahuah more than I need a wife.

I love Elohiym more than I love my wife.

I desire the Lord Almighty more than I desire a wife.

I live for my Heavenly Father before I live for my wife.

I obey the commands of the Most High before I comply with my wife's demands or suggestions.

I serve my Heavenly Father first I serve my wife second.

Do you get the picture children?

The God of Israel comes first!

Second, I love my wife as myself.

I love her like Yahusha loved the church.

I do not deal treacherously with her.

I do not blame her for my disobedience.

I do not deal harshly with her.

I am not unfaithful to my wife.

My wife does not have to work if she doesn't want to.

I love my wife as my own body.

After all no one ever hated their own body.

Don't you feed and care for your body?

My wife is my companion and my partner.

I dwell with her according to knowledge.

Together we inherit His grace, and our prayers are not ineffective.

And in all ways, I seek guidance, knowledge, understanding and wisdom from Yahuah on how to love my wife and family.

Psalms 27

I am not being punished. I am being disciplined.

I am being trained to be more like my Heavenly Father Yahuah.

He is saying to me "let Me show you how to do this."

He is tired of seeing me fail when I go my own way.

He has revealed to me mysteries about myself that I didn't know and mysteries about others.

His discipline feels unpleasant, but I will not lose heart.

If anything, I take it all in joy because He has received me as a son.

And I know after the discipline, which is temporary, I will be blessed.

I will be renewed and restored. My joy will overflow.

I will be exalted because I have been humbled. So I take courage because He loves me so much.

Your current and momentary affliction is not punishment.

Punishment is from the evil one.

He wants to punish you, to steal your joy, to kill you and take your life.

The enemy doesn't want you to learn and progress to the next level. He wants to punish you. Forever.

Thank Yah we have power over all the enemy through the Word His son Yahusha.

For it is written, who shall bring any charge against Elohiym's elect?

It is Elohiym who justifies. If he has justified me the enemy cannot convict me.

And when my temporary discipline is finished, my joy will be complete, and I will be filled with new life and a new spirit!

Psalms 28

Whatever you worry about is something you haven't given to God.

God doesn't want you to worry son.

God doesn't want you to worry daughter.

The enemy is planting fear in your mind.

We overcome fear with faith!

God wants you to focus on Him and give that situation to Him fully so He can fight on your behalf.

Trust Him.

He will not let you be put to shame.

He knows you are in distress.

When you are distressed, He is distressed.

So take courage [grab it, hold onto it, aggressively pursue courage] and be at ease of heart with peace.

God is on my side! Elohiym is on your side!

He will intervene in your troubles on your behalf!

The Lord will save you from the shame, disgrace and the humiliation you fear.

Do not be afraid; do not fear, for I am with you He says.

Do not be dismayed, for I am your God. I will strengthen you and help you.

I will uphold you with my righteous right hand!

Believe in His word child, not in your fear.

Psalms 29 (The King's Decree)

A king makes a decree, and it is carried out

He does not lose sleep or worry wondering if his decree will come to pass

He's a king!

It is written, thou shalt also decree a thing, and it shall be established unto thee: and the light shall shine upon thy ways.

I decree that every generational curse over my family be lifted this day.

I decree that I am the head and not the tail.

I decree that I am on top and not the bottom.

I decree that I am the lender and not the borrower.

I decree that my future is filled with peace and prosperity.

I decree that no weapon formed against me shall prosper.

I decree that I will dwell in the house of Yahuah forever!

I decree that faith has conquered fear in my life.

I decree that my enemies shall fall by the waist side.

I decree that every evil spirit that tries to stand against me be banished and bound in the name of Yahusha Hamaschiach.

I decree that I have dominion and influence.

I decree that the Elohiym of peace will soon crush satan under my feet.

I decree that every Hebrew boy, girl, man and woman return to studying the law, statutes and commandments of Yahuah.

I decree that everyone who reads this be filled with joy and love.

I decree that everyone who reads this be renewed in his or her spirit and life.

I decree that mercy triumph over judgment.

I decree that justice triumph over racism.

I decree that poverty ends in our communities.

I decree that abuse of all kinds end in our communities.

I decree that every spirit of depression, anxiety and fear be bound and banished in the name of Yahusha among all the nations.

We are a peculiar people, a royal priesthood.

He has said, Israel is my firstborn son; let my son go so he may worship Me.

I decree an end to violence amongst brothers and sisters.

I decree an end to the spirit of ignorance and lack of knowledge.

I decree a new beginning for wisdom to fall fresh on our hearts and the Ruach Ha'qodesh (Holy Spirit) fill us and teach us the Law of Yah.

This is the king's decree.

So be it.

Psalms 30

Yahuah Elohiym is my companion.
He is my friend when I am lonely.
He is my best friend.
He keeps me company when I am alone.
He chases my anxiety away.
He chases my fear away.
He puts a new song in my mouth to sing.
A song of praise worship and gratefulness for the great things He hath done and will do.
He has covered me on the shelter of His wings.
All of my help comes from Yah.
No other help I know.
He has set me up in a large space.
He has removed the shame, embarrassment and disgrace of my foolishness.
The dread I feared He has freed me from.
He pitied me when I was in distress.
He saw me as a lost sheep that had lost his way.

He let me stay lost only long enough for me to learn a lesson

Then in His great compassion for me, I heard Him call my name.

And I began to look for Him.

I turned around when I heard His voice.

I said to myself, my Master is calling.

My heart leaped for joy.

The good Shepherd is calling me home.

Though I was a stubborn sheep, I was a disobedient sheep, a prideful sheep.

I am still His sheep.

And I will never follow a stranger

In fact, I will run away from him because I do not recognize a stranger's voice

He gives me eternal life, and no one can snatch me from His hand.

Psalms 31 (A good soldier)

Praise Yahuah Elohaynu
Let everything that hath breath praise Him!
He has done great things.
Halleluyah! You have won the victory.
And I have the victory through you.
You are my Captain, my General, and my Commanding Officer
I follow your orders. I wait for your command.
I show you reverence and salute you.
I am not an insubordinate soldier
I march to the beat of your drum.
Adonai is a man of war. Yahuah is his name!
You have taught my hands to war.
You have taught me combat in spiritual war.
You have told me we war not against the flesh

but against rulers and authorities in the Heavenly realms

War broke out in Shamayim

Michael and his angels fought against the dragon, and the dragon and his angels fought back.

But they were not strong enough and they lost their place in Shamayim

Halleluyah. Death where is thy sting grave where is thy victory.

Though an army come against me I will not be afraid.

Elohiym will hide me in the shelter of his wings

He bends Yahudah like a bow and fills it with Eprhaim.

I am not afraid.

I really am not afraid.

I do not fear.

Like my Father, I am a mighty warrior.

My faith is in Him.

Psalms 32 (Choose for yourselves this day whom you will serve)

If you not blessing someone, you're cursing them

If you ever feel lost it means the Lord is looking for you.

Why do I say this?

Because the Shepherd looks for his sheep when they are lost.

If you not choosing life, you're choosing death

You're either a servant of Yah or a servant to the devil.

You're either worshiping Yah or worshiping the devil

No one can serve two masters. You will either love one or hate the other.

It's pointless to run from God.

Why?

The answer is simple.   There's nowhere to go.

Where are you gonna go to hide from Him?

What hiding place have you found that He does not know of?

Tell me child of God so that I may see this place.

Sex without a covenant with Elohiym (fornication, adultery, masturbation) invites and gives permission for evil spirits to come in and posses you or the person you're having sex with.

Sex under a covenant with Elohiym invites the ruach ha'qodesh to come into your lives and bless your marriage covenant with Elohiym.

Selah...

Remember you are either living a life for the Spirit.

Or you are living your life to indulge the flesh.

The flesh wars against the Spirit and the Spirit wars against the flesh

They are in constant conflict with one another

They struggle fiercely against each other

That which you feed you will serve

This is how you know whether what a person

is saying is from a spirit of truth or a spirit of falsehood concerning Christ.

If a person is saying something that Christ would say of himself then it is from the spirit of truth and that person has the mind of Christ or the spirit of Christ living in them

If a person is saying something that is not something Christ would say about himself then it is a spirit of deceit and a lie.

Test the spirits

You have to listen to what people say. And you will know if they are a child of God or a child of the devil.

If they have gone the way of Cain

Psalms 33

I will live to see the salvation of YAHUAH
I have made Him my refuge.
He commands his angels concerning me
They guard me in all my ways
They lift me up so I don't dash my foot against a stone.
Salvation
Do you know what that word means!
Deliverance from sin and its consequences
Deliverance from harm, ruin or loss. It is redemption.
I am being saved from sin, evil and my error.
YAHUAH is my salvation.
YAHUSHA means YAHUAH saves!
Praise YAHUAH ELOHIYM TSEVA'OTH
I do not know what the end will be.
I do not know how He will do it. I do know I will see His salvation.

Despite my error, despite myself, despite my disobedience

He loves me so much; he will redeem me and show me His yeshu'ah.

He will do it not for me but for his namesake.

So that His name will not be profaned amongst the gentiles.

He will do it so I will know that he is YAHUAH my ELOHIYM and by His might alone have I been saved from my sin, from my foolishness and disobedience.

He is on the rescue mission now! He is resolving my problems right now.

As He has fixed my problems for me in the past He will fix it again.

Just as He showed the Israelites his might and power delivering them from Egypt

Showing them His plagues

Showing them how He parted the Red Sea and they crossed on dry land

He hardened pharoah's heart towards Mosheh, so He would get the glory!

So that He could show his children his awesome and terrible power!

And that for generations the descendants of Yasher'al would know it was Him. YAHUAH TSEVA'OTH who delivered them.

He is my salvation. Of whom shall I fear?

I am not afraid because I trust Him.

I am being made perfect in His love. To learn that perfect love cast out fear.

Love that comes from ELOHIYM is not a love that punishes.

That is not love child of God. Love that comes from ELOHIYM forgives!

It is a love of mercy, grace and salvation!

HalleluYah! HalleluYah! HalleluYah!

Psalms 34 (Final Exhortation)

My heart bleeds internally
My soul cries and I cannot stop it
I have fallen.
Like my name means, I have descended
I was on a high place and I fell down
I could not hear the voice of YAHUAH ELOHAYNU
A spirit of fear had possessed me
YAH warns a man in a dream. In visions in the night
To keep him from falling into the pit. Though no man perceives it.
I did not perceive it. I feel like Esau.
I traded my inheritance for a bowl of savory stew.

I was cast upon YAHUAH from my mother's breast

He taught me to trust in Him from the womb

My father told me before I became a man "to whom much is given much is expected, you will not be able to do the things you see your friends do"

At the time I thought, be quiet old man

Now I see, his words were true like the gospel.

When did I ask for this responsibility?

When did I ask for these great expectations?

I never did, as the pot does not dictate to the Potter on how to mold it.

Before I had a will, before I had a decision, before I had plans for my life, YAHUAH had designed me for His will.

YAHUAH TSEVA'OTH knows the plans of man, that they are futile.

I had my own plans; I laid the groundwork for my future for what I thought was good.

And with a breath of His nostril, He confused my language like the Tower of Babel.

He said, my servant Jared will not succeed in his schemes

For I know the plans I have for him, plans to prosper him and not harm him.

He tore me from the comfort of my friends.

He tore me from the bosom of my woman.

He tore me from my dwelling that I had known all these years.

Every familiar thing He ripped from my clutch.

Then He taught me His name.

Then He taught me His Torah.

Then He showed me my power.

It seemed like wrath to me all the while. It felt like punishment

Then I remember YAHUAH chastens those He accepts as children.

Lover and friend, He put far from me, my brothers he put far into darkness.

He needed my full attention.

I was a soldier who went AWOL. I had forgotten my mission.

I was sent down to do great works.

So, this is my final exhortation to my brethren.

Seek YAHUAH ELOHAYKEM with all your heart, mind, body and soul.

Ask for wisdom, He will surely give it to you.

Learn His Torah. His law, statutes and commandments.

Understand we are to practice them. They are eternal.

They do not make us righteous. It is our obedience to them AND our faith in YAHUSHA that makes us righteous.

Do you not know? By your words you will be acquitted and by your words you will be condemned.

YAHUSHA himself taught from the Torah. So did Paul, even though Paul made it seem like the law was useless.

Know this for certain, sin is lawlessness.

He who sins practices lawlessness. He who does not sin practices righteousness.

You don't even know what sin is, if you don't know the Law.

Observe the Shabbat (Sabbath).

Do not slander or gossip.

Do not use dishonest scales.

Do not deceive your Israelite brother or sister.

Do not lend and charge interest.

Do not avenge your neighbor but treat them as yourself.

Cursed is the one who treats his father or mother with contempt.

Cursed is the one who attacks his neighbor secretly.

Cursed is the one who perverts justice due to the stranger, the fatherless and widow.

Love YAHUAH with all your heart, mind, body and soul.

Do not eat any detestable thing.

After you have harvested your crops (gotten all you need) and see some harvest leftover, leave it for the poor and the needy so they may eat.

Observe the Passover.

Observe the Feast of Unleavened Bread.

The law, statutes and decrees of YAHUAH are so wonderful.

YAHUSHA said as much, take and learn from me, my yoke is easy, and my burden is light.

Stop running child of Elohiym. Return to YAHUAH ELOHAYKA.

The gift of eternal life is in His son YAHUSHA HA' MASHIACH

The pleasures of the world seem very enticing in the moment.

They are fleeting and not real. They fade away.

It is a mirage. The gift of eternal life is just that. Eternal.

www.ingramcontent.com/pod-product-compliance
Lightning Source LLC
Chambersburg PA
CBHW071020080526
44587CB00015B/2438